February 26, 2015

Dear A_____ ught
this little book many years
ago for you—when you were
going to have your "first child"
I thought I would send it
along now. Even though your
"first" is not here with us
all today, you and Brian
have become a "Mom" and "Dad"
a child who passed away into
heaven

at a very young age; but now, you are the "Mom and Dad" of a "precious little angel" who has gone home; and, is now in a "perfect state of Glory" with The Dear Lord in Heaven!! Wow, what a privilege for you both — and one day, you can all be re-united — I am looking forward to that someday my self to meet my very first grandchild !!

~ With My Love ~

Mom xxoo

It's a mom's life!

written and illustrated by
Emily Williams-Wheeler.

Adventure Publications
Cambridge, Minnesota

Published by
Adventure Publications, Inc.
P.O. Box 269
Cambridge, MN 55008

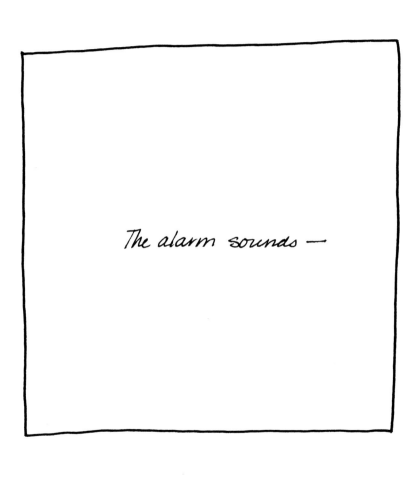

The alarm sounds —

a response is expected

and needs must be met.

There are often challenges

and patience is continually tried.

With a kiss and a wave,
new adventures begin

despite a minor setback.

Going miles for one

means another must wait.

Before long the regular
work pace resumes.

The clock races,

personal moments are devoured.

Working together, goals are attained

and individual triumphs recognized.

There are little stops along the way,

but home is where the heart is.

A team effort is made

to make the most of family time.

Sailing in and out of imagination,

a dreamy peace snuggles in.

After sorting through
the events of the day

and collecting one's self,

the comforts of home
are finally realized.

The promise is a gift now

to keep..

For more information
on books by
Emily Williams-Wheeler,
contact your local
gift / book store or
Adventure Publications
1·800·678·7006.